Never Assume

PATRICIA MCGUIRE, MD FAAP

Never Assume

Getting To Know Children
Before Labeling Them

Published by Advantage, Charleston, South Carolina.
Member of Advantage Media Group.

ADVANTAGE is a registered trademark and the Advantage colophon is a trademark of Advantage Media Group, Inc.

Printed in the United States of America.

ISBN: 978-159932-392-3
LCCN: 2013930273

This publication is designed to provide accurate and authoritative information in regard to the subject matter covered. It is sold with the understanding that the publisher is not engaged in rendering legal, accounting, or other professional services. If legal advice or other expert assistance is required, the services of a competent professional person should be sought.

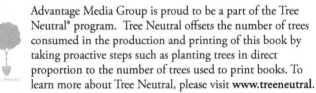

Advantage Media Group is proud to be a part of the Tree Neutral® program. Tree Neutral offsets the number of trees consumed in the production and printing of this book by taking proactive steps such as planting trees in direct proportion to the number of trees used to print books. To learn more about Tree Neutral, please visit **www.treeneutral. com**. To learn more about Advantage's commitment to being a responsible steward of the environment, please visit **www. advantagefamily.com/green**

Advantage Media Group is a leading publisher of business, motivation, and self-help authors. Do you have a manuscript or book idea that you would like to have considered for publication? Please visit **www.advantagefamily.com** or call **1.866.775.1696**

ACKNOWLEDGEMENTS

I would like to thank all of my mentors, colleagues, and friends throughout the years, who have helped me become the type of person I want to be. I learned from my high school chemistry teacher, Mr. Swanson, the meaning of the word *assume*, which has stood me in good stead over the decades. Sister Mary (aka Sister Louie) taught me that respect goes both ways. She also taught me not to take myself too seriously, or else I would miss some of the joy in life. Charlie Cannon, my Chaucer professor, showed me that integrity needs to be maintained even in the face of bureaucracy. Charles Lindsay and Stan Watkins, also professors at Coe, showed me the importance of watching my audience to make sure they understood what I was trying to convey to them. Dr. Dennis O'Connell demonstrated that one can and should always remember the child within the diagnosis. To several staff physicians at Mayo Clinic who demonstrated that one must stand up for the underdog and not let injustice perpetuate itself, I thank you. To the many developmental and behavioral pediatricians who blazed the trail for our specialty, I offer my sincerest thanks for allowing me to learn from your wisdom. And to my family who have given me more than enough practice and experience in practicing what I preach to other families, I love you all.

TABLE OF CONTENTS

SECTION I:
TEMPERAMENT

SECTION II:
RESPECT

SECTION III:
ACCEPTING AND LOVING CHILDREN

INTRODUCTION

Children are born wanting to be loved, accepted, and respected. The rest we have to teach them. In order to teach them, however, we must first understand children. They are not little adults. Children are born with a profile of temperament traits that rule how they behave or respond to what is occurring in their environment. These traits, along with life experiences, will mold or develop their personalities. It is our responsibility to guide them through this process, bringing our love, experience, and empathy into the equation.

Beyond temperament, children are also born with a range of strengths and deficits, some relative, and others significantly different. These differences can affect just a small part of their lives or influence how they interact all day long. We, as adults, don't always remember our own childhood differences and how they made us feel. We also now live in a different time, where the hows and whys of children are better understood, rather than just criticized or punished.

There is still a great deal we need to understand better, with science helping us through observation and technology, such as functional MRIs. Stories of children can be a means of letting adults see children from a more objective eye, rather than the subjective eye colored by worry, fear, or frustration.

This book represents what children have taught me over the last 30 years, both my own children and the ones I shared with parents through my practice. They inspired me to buy a plaque for my office that says, "Children are to be seen, heard, and believed." As I now tell the children I see, I am there to be their voice, when others don't understand. I hope you find in the following chapters some answers to the questions you have about your child.

SECTION I

TEMPERAMENT

SECTION I

TEMPERAMENT

This first section will focus on how temperament looks and feels to the parents and the child. I will start with a true story about my first child, who knows this article was first written and published while she was in middle school. I remind her all the time that she taught me so much that allowed us to keep our bond and grow into friends as she grew into a lovely young woman.

The second chapter looks more specifically at how some traits look, and includes suggestions on how to work more effectively with a child exhibiting those temperament traits to a level that creates stress in the parent/child relationship.

It is important to step back and first attempt to observe neutrally what is seen (antecedent environment), what happens at the change (the behavioral incident), and the subsequent consequence (what response is given to the child) to determine if the child was understood correctly or just seen as a disruption to be silenced.

If the consequence does not stop the behavior immediately AND in the future, it was not addressing the how and why of the behavior—the possibility of temperament mismatch as a causative factor. This is when one has to review the possible temperament traits that influenced the child's behavior in order to teach strategies of how to handle it, or if that is impossible due to age and developmental level, how to have the environment accommodate the child's needs until such time as the cognitive skills of the child will allow the learning of strategies. As you read the two chapters you should get a better idea of how this can be done. There are also resources listed in the Appendix which can expand your understanding.

CHAPTER 1

It's More Than
Simple Colic

All during my first pregnancy I prayed for two things: my child to be born healthy, and without colic. Simple requests to God, right? Well, God did indeed answer my prayers, but with a little bit of his "gotcha" sense of humor. Ten days past my due date and almost as a C-section, my daughter was born. She was healthy—nine pounds, one ounce—with a lusty cry. Little did I know what that cry would lead to.

I am a Developmental & Behavioral Pediatrician, so I felt I knew all there was about handling babies. I really felt colic would have been the ultimate disaster for me with my hectic schedule. I didn't realize then about a significantly more important consideration—temperament. I was still under the naive belief that babies were born with a clean slate as far as personality is concerned, molded instead by interactions with the various caretakers.

Fussy babies, poor sleepers, temper tantrums were all totally preventable situations if the parents, especially the mother, used good, consistent parenting techniques. My oldest child taught me differently, leading to my fascination with temperament.

Temperament consists of the core personality traits we are all born with. These traits are inherited, just as height potential, eye color, and hair color are inherited. After birth, they begin to be modified—for better or worse—by the infant's interactions with the various members of her environment. Basically, how others react to her reactions or responses in a situation lead to a feeling of competence and satisfaction by all parties, or anger and frustration.

THE 9 TRAITS OF TEMPERAMENT ARE:

1. *Activity Level* – If no one tells you to hurry up or slow down, when are you most comfortable? This is your own cruising speed through life.

2. *Rhythmicity* – This is how well your inside clock matches up with the outside clock of the world. It affects sleep and wake cycles, hunger, and elimination. It also affects organization and time management since it helps in the feeling of the passage of time.

3. *Distractability* – This can also be described as the division of attention. It looks at the ability to focus on what is important and still be aware of the world around you.

4. *Approachability/Withdrawl* – This describes how quickly or slowly one adapts to different people, places, and situations.

5. *Attention Span & Persistence* – This is how easy or hard it is to start and complete a task. Some individuals need assistance due to problems with motivation and some due to a low frustration tolerance. Others are very good at persisting at one or a multitude of activities simultaneously.

6. *Intensity of Reactions* – This is how much a person's emotional change is noted from

moment to moment. Some people are light switches, being all of one emotion or another. Others have a broad range of emotional responses to situations.

7. *Adaptability* – This is the ease with which a person adapts to change in his environment. Some people always go with the flow, while others get bent out of shape if there is any unexpected change in the routine.

8. *Threshold of Responsiveness* – This is the intensity of stimulation required for a person to show a discernible response. How tuned are they into what is going on around them at that moment—are they like the Princess and the Pea, or more like the guy sitting in San Francisco, missing the earthquake?

9. *Quality of Mood* – This is the amount of friendly, pleasant, joyful behavior as contrasted with unpleasant, unfriendly behavior. Basically, is the person a cloud finder or a silver-lining finder?

I now know that my daughter is intense in her reactions and has a basically negative mood. In the newborn nursery, the staff would comment on the abruptness of her awakening and intense crying. She sounded like a child-abuse victim when I changed her diaper. She was very against the concept of breastfeeding, appearing to think I was trying to choke or poison her. It took the entire three days of my postpartum stay, with a lot of nursing staff assistance, for her to finally settle into the idea of breastfeeding. Unfortunately, it wasn't until I was ready for discharge that my milk came in. A friend brought us home since my husband had to work. Totally alone at home with my daughter, I began to fear for her health. She again was refusing to breastfeed since the situation had changed. I was so engorged it was hard to latch on, and when she did, a large quantity of milk would seemingly attack her. It was 20 below zero outside, so there was no chance of some wise mother/friend coming to hold my hand. My own mother had bottle-fed us, so she, also long-distance, was of no help. Finally, after going about nine hours with only sips of nourishment, my child relented and began nursing from my rock-hard breasts.

As time elapsed, I came to experience the other aspects of her temperament; literally needing 20 minutes of solitude, with much crying, to adjust to the event of sleeping; extreme sensitivities to taste and texture, which meant that until middle school we had to negotiate with her as to which tags could be snipped out of her clothes and which had to stay due to special cleaning instructions; negative first impressions to almost everything (I never knew how far an infant could stick out its tongue in response to the first taste of green beans); very flamboyant displays of whichever emotion she was experiencing at the moment; and the room-destroying temper tantrums. By the time she was two years old, I was convinced she had been born with permanent PMS. It was then that I came to the conclusion that I either had to find a different style of parenting, which would allow us to co-exist in relative harmony—or kill her.

Since my daughter is now a college graduate, in her early 20s , it is obvious as to my decision and its success. That's not to say life has been a bowl full of cherries—well, maybe it has as long as you accept the pits, too—but by understanding temperament and "goodness of fit," I have been able to look through her eyes and walk in her shoes more, allowing better conflict resolution, rather than assuming she was intentionally sabotaging situations.

Goodness of fit is another term for compatibility. It describes the interaction of the strengths and characteristics of the child with the demands and expectations of the environment (i.e., the parents and other caretakers). Compatibility takes work on both sides, through negotiation and compromise. With infants and small children, however, it is more of a one-way street. The caretakers must use their skills to keep the relationship evolving in a positive direction. This requires slowing down to analyze how the child is responding to the situation or environment. One needs to look both at what is known of the child's temperamental pattern and at environmental influences such as the child's health, if he's hungry or tired, or for any causes of decreased frustration tolerance, such as overstimulating surroundings (i.e., grocery stores or family gatherings). This forced me to slow down my own reaction rate and consider possible reasons for her behavior and my options for response. Long ago I discarded phrases from my own childhood ("If you are going to cry, I will give you a reason to cry" and "Do it because I say so") which don't recognize the stress my daughter was encountering in her interactions with the environment. By learning how to recognize the hows of her actions and responses, I feel I became better able to teach my daughter problem-solving skills, self-calming skills, and interpersonal communication skills. She has matured into a delightful young lady as a result of my efforts, with a very healthy self-esteem.

You can develop these skills, too, with a lot of practice, patience (for your own temperament), and the realization that this is a long-term goal (I've been learning and relearning these skills for 20+ years). Understanding and working with her temperament allowed me to grow with my daughter and no longer see her as at risk for homicide or at least foster-care.

CHAPTER 2

Is There A Little Witch In Your House?

"There she goes again, howling like a banshee," moans Angie to her neighbor Julie. "Whenever Megan doesn't get her way, she throws blood-curdling temper tantrums. I can't take her anywhere without forewarning. She refuses to go with the flow. And talk about picky! It's a daily nightmare getting her dressed. She complains that her socks' seams hurt. Her shirt tags have been cut out because they scratch her back. I won't tell you about her eating habits. When I was pregnant, I dreamt of having a little princess, but I've been cursed with a witch."

Did Angie's mother curse her with the phrase, "May you have a child just like you"? Some children make their parents feel as if they're under an evil spell. Children aren't supposed to be so difficult to raise. Why can't Angie, and other parents like her, find the magic to make their children happy, obedient, and self-confident?

For the last 40+ years, behavioral specialists have been studying temperament to supply reasons for these conflicts. Temperament is the child's style of reacting to her world. There are nine traits of temperament making up the child's personality, inherited from their parents. These traits are then further molded by interactions with their parents and other caretakers.

Let's look at Megan's traits and learn how to dispel the potential conflicts between Angie and her child:

APPROACHABILITY/WITHDRAWAL

Megan is very withdrawn, clinging to Angie's side, needing extended warm-up time before she'll get involved with new kids. Angie can decrease her frustration with Megan by:

- Talking her through the process of viewing situations and people; discussing the safety or level of danger before joining in.

- Allowing Megan time to ease into the situation, staying at her side, or sitting next to her (not holding her or letting her sit on your lap). Once Megan's comfortable, she will join her peer group.

ADAPTABILITY

Angie wants Megan to go with the flow. Megan, however, has difficulties handling transitions due to feelings of anxiety. Angie wants Megan to be a Porsche, capable of changing gears rapidly. Megan, however, is a semi-truck, needing to shift many gears before she can start a new activity. To help Megan learn transition skills, Angie needs to:

- Give advance warning of a new event or needed change. This will allow Megan time to determine how to stop what she's doing in order to start something else.

- Angie and Megan should keep a schedule to anticipate changes during the day. They can use a toy clock with changeable hands, or a paper chain, each link naming an activity. The links are taken off as a new activity is started.

INTENSITY OF REACTIONS

Megan is very intense in her reactions, always wearing her emotions on her sleeve. Megan would benefit from learning techniques of body language:

- Angie can either buy or make a poster showing different facial expressions. She and Megan can play games, having Megan decide which face matches how Angie is acting.

- Angie should check with Megan during the day to see what she's feeling. At first, this should be a game, to avoid making Megan feel self-conscious. Megan should also ask Angie to check her feelings, allowing Megan to check her interpretation.

- Angie could have Megan work with a behavioral specialist, learning relaxation techniques and allowing her to be more in charge of her emotions.

- Megan may enjoy role-playing, giving her practice in modifying her emotions.

THRESHOLD OF RESPONSIVENESS

Angie is frustrated by Megan's low sensory threshold—needing clothes to feel just right, being slow to accept new foods because they don't taste, smell, or feel right. Megan also claims that Angie yells all the time, being very sensitive to tone of voice and body language. To help Megan, Angie needs to:

- Give Megan time to adjust to new clothing, washing them before they're worn if stiffness bothers her. Angie can sew tags down completely to decrease movement if they can't be removed.

- Present a new food at several meals over a few weeks, having Megan only taste it, with her favorite foods present to balance the meal out. Over time she will possibly tolerate the food, but if not, accept that we each have individual tastes.

- Check with Megan as to how she hears voice levels, words, facial expressions, etc., helping her to see it in a different light.

QUALITY OF MOOD

Megan's first reaction to any announcement is frustration and anger. She's allowed a first impression, but it frustrates Angie to hear the negatives. Basically, Megan is a cloud finder, requiring Angie to realize that she needs to learn to not argue or get angry. Everyone has an impression, but by arguing it, Megan won't be allowed to have a less negative second impression. Angie needs to acknowledge that it seems awful to Megan, but that she will check back with her as Megan gets into it, to see how she is doing.

Working to understand Megan's temperament traits (and her own) will allow Angie to accept different ways of approaching situations, the need to give space, to provide forewarnings, and consider alternatives. Like Angie, as you and your child work together, you will find that the spell has been lifted, releasing the princess within your witch.

SECTION II

RESPECT

SECTION II

RESPECT

As was mentioned in the beginning, children are born wanting to be loved, accepted, and respected. They don't know what these look like, but can feel it when they experience them: hugs, kisses, smiles when they are seen, having their needs met for food and human contact, and staying comfortable through clothes and diaper changes. They don't know how to reciprocate because they can't show the exact actions until they grow older. All they can do is look at us and settle in our arms, and sleep the sleep of the contented and secure.

The first chapter will look at how children are taught respect through our actions, the ways to respond to others, and how we as adults need to monitor our actions in order for children to be able to model respectful behavior. They can't do what they have never seen or experienced.

The second chapter reveals the need we still have to understand the concept of love, acceptance, and respect through the story of the polar opposite. It is based closely on the events of a friend of mine. The sad thing is that it occurred just recently, even though we all feel that we have learned how to respect individuals with disabilities as people with potential.

The third chapter looks at the problem of learning disabilities and how we must not allow the media to make fun of those who struggle to learn.

The fourth chapter looks at how we must show our children we respect them by meaning what we say and saying what we mean. Too many times we take back what we said if it is inconvenient for us, which sends the message to our children that we don't respect their time, their ability to make choices and decisions, and their right to learn from their experiences how life works.

CHAPTER 1

First We Must Respect Them

The Roberts family arrived for their counseling session emanating anger and frustration before the first word was spoken. "I am sick and tired of Josh and Sara disobeying the rules," stated Mrs. Roberts. Mr. Roberts added, "They ignore us unless we get into their faces, lipping off when they do finally respond to us. We're their parents and deserve more respect."

Sound familiar? In physician and therapists' offices across the country, this same scene takes place, often several times per day. Parents feel helpless to control their kids, to elicit respect from them. What's going wrong? Was it so different in past generations, as we frequently hear?

Looking back, parents most likely didn't get respect from their children as much as fear. The physical aggression that took place would quickly land a parent in jail today, with the child being placed in foster care. It never lasted, however, with an eventual rebellion, usually by the son, finally growing big enough to fight back and win, thus establishing a new relationship.

Parents no longer see corporal punishment as a viable means of raising their kids, but don't have another model to follow. This, in addition to the increase of job demands, self-fulfillment demands, and technology changes, has created our present dilemma. Kids demand our time and attention, much like weeds or mosquitoes. Contrary to our subjective belief, however, they aren't doing it to add chaos to our lives. Rather, they are trying to feel secure and loved, and to learn how to grow up. We are their primary role models, just as our parents were our role models. If we complain that our children don't follow the rules and don't show us respect, we need to ask, "Are we first modeling these behaviors to our children?" Most often, the answers are "Sometimes," or "I go by different rules since I am the parent," or "I won't show them respect until they've earned it by showing me respect."

In order to expect children to function within our society's expectations, we need to change our view of our role in child-rearing. We have to think about

- The age and developmental level of the child

- What are absolute rules

- What are flexible rules

- What does "respect" look like, sound like, feel like

Many parents today show anger and frustration with infants who cry in public or have rough times in the evening. They need help understanding the ideas of routine, consistency, and the reasons why an infant is acting contrary. Basic child development has shown that:

- Newborns and infants spend most of their days and nights sleeping in one- to three-hour stretches. When they are forced to stay awake, they frequently become irritable, with crying and squirming.

- As they reach the end of the first year, they may become more physical with grabbing, scratching, hitting, and biting when tired, hungry, or ill.

- Toddlers and preschoolers are trying to learn independence and begin to check limits by doing what they are told not to.

- School age children are working to understand their place in society and how to incorporate what they are learning in school with what they have been taught at home.

- Adolescents are going through a second stage of pushing for independence, defining who they are and what they believe in.

These developmental needs of children have to be approached with calm, cool logic. We as the parents must pause, assess what events led up to this moment based on facts, not presumptions, determine how (and when) to discuss with our child the events, and have options for consequences for the outcome. Consistency with regard to expectations, including the positive and negative consequences that the child can expect from their actions, is essential. Having family meetings on a regular basis can be helpful, as well as having lists and visual reminders throughout the house for chores or activities that have created problems in the past. Frequently talking with our children about their days, discussing how you handle frustration or the need to work with people you don't care for, will provide some of the modeling they need.

Remember, you wouldn't want your boss or supervisor to treat you the way you treat your children, so you need to treat your children the way you expect to be treated.

So how does respect look? How does respect sound? These are vital questions that we must ask ourselves as we prepare to interact with children.

Starting with infants, we need to use the type of voice that reflects our acceptance of their being in our world. It is fine to use baby talk and rhythmic talking as we work to get and maintain their attention. When they are fussing, however, we must approach them as we would an upset customer or coworker. Using the voice of concern, which is lower and more soothing in nature, we go through the possibilities of what might be bothering them as we check out those same areas. An example would be "You are not happy. Do you need your diaper changed?" This also helps you to remember that for a baby, crying or fussing, as vague as it may be, is the only means they have of communicating. You can model both language and empathy to the infant.

With toddlers and preschoolers, oral language becomes more important, but more so are the nonverbal components of communication. Little children will be more concrete and literal, frequently understanding only the words and not the tone of voice or facial expressions. This leads to many of the confused responses that the adults receive where a child will be scolded, but laughs in response. They also will only comprehend the concrete meaning of words, so figurative language, such as idioms, metaphors, and analogies, will go over their head. An example would be asking a fidgety child if he has *ants in his pants.*

When communicating with toddlers and pre-schoolers, always get down to their eye level; do not expect them to look up to you, which stresses them physically. It is not always important to have eye contact, and, in fact, forcing it frequently causes them to lose focus on the message. While at eye level with them, use a low, calm voice, saying their name first with a pause, before focusing on the reason for the conversation. Keep the words simple with few adjectives. Each sentence should be five to six words or less, if possible. Add emotion words to help them learn to relate actions and body language with what the other person (or they) might be feeling. An example would be "Joey's sad that you hit him. He doesn't know why you did. Can you say why?"

As children enter school, our role is to become a sounding board, which means listening, repeating back at times what was heard, and checking on the correctness of what was heard. Children and adolescents are trying to make sense of differences they are encountering outside of the home, from interactions with their peers, teachers, and others. As parents we can help them try to step into that person's shoes, to think about the how or why of the other's actions or words. This is teaching them perspective and problem-solving, which are needed as one develops skills of respect. Brainstorming of possible reasons for another's actions or words should be without censor, allowing all possibilities to be listed. When that is done, one can then go through the list with the child and ask if it fits with events before or after the situation, or with the person as previously known. Frequently it is good to put the brainstorming on paper to allow the visualization of the process, which increases the understanding of how to solve problems. This would be much like doing an outline before writing a report or book, or a grocery list so no item is forgotten.

As we pay attention to how we present ourselves to our children, much like we monitor how we do this with our boss or customers, we will see an increase in the respectful behaviors in our children. In the end, we have to remember that children do as we do, not as we say, so we need to do what we want them to do.

CHAPTER 2

Shining Star, How I Wonder Where You Are

She was a very special young girl. Her parents knew this before she was born. They looked forward to her birth, aware that she would need their help, but would also give them a special understanding of the magic of life. They named her Star, since she was the shining star of their love.

She had some initial health concerns when she was born, but proved that she had the heart and spirit to live. Her parents reveled in the strength of determination she exhibited, healing from the surgery. She had other childhood illnesses, but nothing serious, bouncing back as most children would.

She required longer than normal to master many developmental skills. She was able, however, to walk down the aisle as a flower girl at age three when her brothers got married. She also had a flare for dancing, which she did almost daily at home and school. She had difficulties in the pronunciation of words. This didn't stop her from talking to friends, singing, and voicing her opinion and feelings.

She was a friend to all, giving hugs to those she met each day. She was kind to those in need, and was eager to learn with the help of others. She developed good horse-riding skills, even winning some ribbons. She competed with classmates at four-square during recess. She glowed when playing with her nephews and niece. She added brilliance to the lives of others she encountered.

One day she began to cough and developed a fever. Initially she was treated at home with antibiotics. After a few more days, she was not improving, and in fact began to struggle to breathe. She was hospitalized for pneumonia in the local hospital. She was receiving good care but was struggling with her breathing.

The covering physician was uncomfortable with her degree of respiratory struggle and decided to transfer her to a tertiary medical center. Before her transfer, Star was getting a lot of attention from the nurses and respiratory staff, being encouraged to get out of bed to use the bathroom and stretch her legs. After she was rushed via helicopter to the tertiary center, she was put into diapers and confined to her bed. She was attached to many machines, with a mask over her face at all times. She was not allowed to eat or drink because of the mask. After several days, when the parents refused to have a tube put through her nose to her stomach or surgically placed into her stomach, the physicians began giving her nutrition through an IV line.

Star fussed a lot due to her fear and frustration at not being able to move around. This caused her heart rate to increase and her oxygenation to decrease. The doctors, however, interpreted it as increasing complications from her pneumonia and her heart. They did multiple tests, eventually withdrawing so much blood that they had to give her a blood transfusion. The parents had to fight to get her therapy dog into the room to calm her down, which did help.

Several days after being transferred, friends from her school came to visit and noted that she wasn't using her left hand, and the left side of her face looked different. The parents also began to notice these changes, but it wasn't until several days later that the doctors and nurses also noted it and began to explore why she had had a stroke.

They alternately blamed it on the pneumonia and her heart, although the latter had received a clean bill of health from the heart specialist only a couple of days before. The doctors didn't seem too upset about the stroke, asking finally if Star had ever been mobile. They had been busy, so had never taken the time to get to know Star.

The doctors were adamant that she needed more tests, and a tonsil surgery, but the parents refused the latter, since they knew it wasn't her tonsils that were causing the oxygen problems, but rather the anxiety, which did improve, along with the oxygen levels, when they finally gave her medication to calm her.

The day after the doctors acknowledged the stroke, Star developed unexpected breathing problems, leading to a respiratory arrest and eventually death. She had experienced a pulmonary embolism from her legs, which is a common problem with people who are on prolonged bed rest, with lack of movement of the extremities. The parents had to fight to avoid an autopsy and to stay with their daughter until the funeral home picked her up.

Star's visitation was a time of remembering all the goodness of her. She had touched hundreds of people. Staff from the local hospital came to pay their last respects too, since Star had touched their lives even in the short time she had been under their care. There was no representative from the tertiary center.

They had missed the opportunity to know the joy of Star. All who have known Star are appreciative of the experience. Now we suspect she is sharing her love of life in heaven too.

CHAPTER 3

Learning Disabilities Are No Laughing Matter

An editorial cartoon was faxed to me several years ago. On page 10A of *The Des Moines Register*, September 15, 1997, a university administrator was talking with a potential student. The student informed the administrator that he had a "learning disability." The accommodating administrator replied that services were available, and asked about his specific disability. The next scene shows the student saying, "I'm lazy." The person faxing me found the cartoon insulting, having a son with significant learning disabilities, who struggled daily to keep up with his class. I found it insulting, not only to that young person, but to the 15-20% of the general population who are known to have learning disabilities, most of whom don't quite make the severity numbers to receive services.

Some students who would qualify for services are never referred for a special education evaluation due to the current education methods of identification. I have worked with many families who, after years of trying, finally manage to persuade the school system to evaluate their child for learning disabilities, as he enters middle school or even high school. Not surprisingly, the student does qualify by all of the mandated criteria. The student, however, doesn't want the help by that late date, feeling that accepting it would confirm that he is dumb. He opts rather to either struggle along with grades that don't reflect the number of hours he pained over an assignment or studied for a test, or to take the class clown or troublemaker role to deflect attention from his disability. After all, it's more face-saving to get in trouble for goofing off, or kicked out of class for being disruptive, than to sit there not knowing how to do an assignment or stumbling over answers when called on.

It isn't all directly the teachers' fault for this. Teachers across the country aren't being taught language development in our colleges and universities, needed to understand how to teach reading and writing. Regular education teachers aren't taught how to assess potential learning difficulties in their students, allowing for earlier referral and education assistance. Frequently, teachers are told by the child study team to go back and try different techniques before the student will be considered for an education evaluation. The increasing sizes of our classes, with minimal teacher assistance, do not allow the teacher a great deal of time to work individually with each student, in order to identify learning difficulties, much less remediate them. Due to financial constraints, students who don't make the cutoff of impairment—roughly two grades below their current level—will get no assistance. Students who are gifted, but due to a learning disability are struggling to keep up to grade level, frequently receive no assistance, since the funding will only support getting all students up to grade level, not to reach their true potential. These students, however, frequently are harassed with, "I know you are bright enough, you're just not applying yourself," and believe, as the cartoon student has labeled himself, "I'm lazy," which is what he was most likely told for years.

The media must be sensitive to special needs populations. They have a special obligation not to imply that people see learning disabilities as a joke.

Far from a joke, it is a national disgrace that we haven't taken seriously enough, leading to the increase of drugs, teen suicide, crime, overcrowded prisons, and underemployed people in our country. The media needs to vow to assist individuals with learning disabilities in their battle for respect for their needs, aid for their untapped potential, and recognition of the value they add to our communities.

CHAPTER 4

We Have To Mean What We Say

"My kids are driving me crazy! They are forever trying to talk their way out of doing something or having me compromise on my decision. They don't accept their punishments without long arguments. Yes, I know I have buckled many times, reducing the punishment or making exceptions to a grounding for special occasions. But I have a right to change my mind if the punishment interferes with *how I need to run my day*."

What's wrong with this picture? First, the parent in question complains that the child won't accept a parental decision or directive. Later, however, the parent admits to voluntarily changing the consequence after it's in effect if it (the consequence) puts a burden on his daily life. The child in this situation learns that what's "final" may not be "final" and there

53

are ways to lessen a negative outcome and get back to enjoying *his daily existence.*

Inconsistencies and multiple exceptions to the rules of daily living are hard for children to understand, much less develop an understanding of responsibility for one's actions. Parents, however, aren't the only ones having a difficult time understanding the importance of this concept of standing by one's rules and decisions. Our judicial system is famous for giving mixed messages to legal offenders. Just think of some of the situations we read about in the paper and hear about on TV—both in the news and in the evening shows such as *Law & Order.* A person is caught red-handed committing a crime. Logic would tell us that there is a standard punishment based on the laws for that crime. In reality, everything is open for negotiation, ranging to pleading guilty to a lesser offense all the way to dismissal of charges if the person agrees to help the police convict someone whom they feel is more of a community threat than the first offender was.

Then there are the daily reports of not enough room in our prisons, so criminals are released sooner, by reduction of sentence for good behavior and/

or parole. Texas recently began deciding to release prisoners sooner due to overcrowding based on the seriousness of their offense. The nonviolent drug abusers and the violent criminals had to stay, but those convicted of fraud, car theft, and other nonviolent offenses would be released back into the community on parole before their time was completed. They are now finding a significant increase in these crimes. What do you want to wager these offenders aren't as worried about re-incarceration? They know that the system will release them early due to a space crunch—no matter what the judge says is the amount of time which they have to serve for their crime.

How can we expect our citizens to obey the law and respect the rights of others when we don't keep our word as to how we will respond in terms of consequences for their actions? How can we expect our children to believe us and learn responsibility if we don't start at home enforcing our policies and rules? Sticking to our beliefs of what is right and wrong does require sacrifice on the part of the person in authority. If he doesn't believe enough in what he is trying to teach his children/citizens to follow through with previously laid out responses to appropriate and inappropriate actions, then it is time to look at those same policies and rules, determine which are really necessary, and discard the rest. He then needs to recommit to enforcing those remaining policies and rules in order to maintain the integrity of the family/society. Without this commitment, we are simply allowing our family/society to exist in chaos and anarchy. The choice is ours—and so is the responsibility for the outcome of that choice. *Choose wisely.*

SECTION III

ACCEPTING AND LOVING CHILDREN

SECTION III

ACCEPTING AND LOVING CHILDREN

As a parent of children with special needs, I found myself many times trying to make my children fit into the mold of the "perfect child." It was never a good fit, since they were not that child—they were themselves. Over time I learned to accept who they were, how they processed life, and how they learned. I learned that they often were able to cut through the "crap" and just deal with a situation, while I, the all-knowing adult, wanted to make more of a situation than it had to be.

I learned from my children, and all the children I have cared for, that we have to find the styles of teaching that best match their styles of learning. This allows them to work on a much more level playing field with their peers than if we force them to learn from a poorly fit curriculum or method. The first three chapters look at these children and some ways that have been helpful to them.

The fourth chapter is a declaration of love that surpasses the struggles of raising a child with special needs. The last chapter brings the greatest gift you can give to the children you live and work with—Time. Providing love and the time needed to succeed, all children have a chance at reaching their dreams.

CHAPTER 1

Explaining The Why Child

By A Former Why Child

As adults, we expect that we will be seen by children as wise, knowledgeable, and sane. Most children will follow our commands, with little or no objection, if they know us, and know they are expected to obey us. There is a small group of children, however, about 15% of the population, who doesn't follow the expectations of hierarchy that have been set up.

These children may go by many labels; stubborn, strong-willed, or more and more often, oppositional and defiant. We, as adults, see it as our duty to reform them into the compliant children that we expect, and prefer. For most of us, however, this becomes an increasingly frustrating experience as they set their heels like a Missouri mule, refusing to comply or follow us until we answer, to their satisfaction,

"Why?" Now as adults, we are under the impression that we don't have to explain ourselves, especially to those individuals who are smaller and younger than we are and whom we are supposed to be in charge of.

First we need to get to know the why child. Temperamentally, this child is most likely slow to adapt to change. He may also be intense in his emotional response and negative in his mood/first impression of most things. He is slow to adapt to change, going through life very ill at ease with the future. He can't stand not having preparation time for what is coming up next. He frequently goes to extreme lengths to coordinate his actions and plans in order to feel less stressed. Adults feel manipulated and controlled by this child, who pushes to do things a certain way or at a certain time. He is seen as bossy to his peers, having to establish the rules himself and getting very upset if someone tries to bring in an exception to a rule.

This child does not have a natural ability to problem-solve and predict from past experiences. He is very literal in his understanding and interpretation of situations and language. He doesn't know how to step into another person's shoes to see things from their perspective. Life is just one surprise after another due to this, with many of the surprises being unpleasant. This is why he is often using some form of the why questions; why me, why now, and why this way.

Adults need to understand the importance of answering the why questions, and how to answer them correctly. A frequent mistake made by adults is to answer a why question with a who answer. The classic is "Why do I have to do this?" "Because I said so" (a who answer). The child will then angrily respond with something like "I know you said to, but why?" The child sees the adult as not being very smart because they don't even understand how to answer a simple question correctly. Due to the stress they feel, they likely don't use social niceties such as a calm, friendly tone of voice, and may quickly come up with negatives as to why the request may be inappropriate (as to the doer, when and how). These are the influences of the temperament traits of intensity of response and negative mood. They are not inherently oppositional and defiant behavior, but they sure feel like it. Unfortunately, if we don't understand the underlying motivations of this child, he could well develop a more permanent oppositional defiant personality.

The hardest part is keeping your cool in order to reflect on his question(s) in order to walk him through the logical sequence of thoughts that led to the choices you made. Many parents have found over the years if they can do this, the child will be more compliant. The ones who struggle with it have difficulty recreating their thought process, or at times just chose that child because he was the closest at the time that the need came up, not because he wasn't already engaged in something, or that he created the problem in the first place. Some parents also go on how their family set up rules that may not apply well to this family, thus having no logical explanation for the child other than "That is the way it was done when I was your age."

In order to help this child, we need to model for him how to work with others, take other's perspectives, and present his needs in a more friendly form of self-advocacy. This can be done by talking to ourselves when we are around them so that they have the opportunity to hear our logical thoughts for ruling in and out options. If they are to be part of the decision, you can then invite them in to discuss some of the steps that would require decisions as to who would do it, when it actually needed to be done, and why one way of doing it would be better than other options. Having paper and pencil on which to plot this out is also helpful, since whether the child can read or not, the concreteness of something in black and white does help them keep to the logic of the process, not the emotion. If possible, small sketches of people with bubbles over their heads (stick people or just heads are acceptable) to represent the conversation will allow them to see the sequence and order of such interactions. This method, along with role playing, is also very useful to helping the child develop friendly forms of self-advocacy.

At times, your child will come to you upset with how he felt he was treated by another—adult or peer—and benefit from the visual problem-solving technique again. In this case, you would have the child think of as many possible reasons for the other person's behavior or response, and then work it backward to what that person may have been thinking or feeling, and what message the child was conveying by his behavior or response. This technique is also a good way to review positive situations, where it appeared as if the child was able to be more adaptable, and help him see if he had guessed at some of the other person's reasons for the difference in beliefs, or need for a change of action.

These children don't want to be seen as mean, spiteful, or manipulative. They are desperate to be accepted. By using these techniques and understanding the "whys" of their behaviors, you can help them reach their goal.

CHAPTER 2

I'd Make A Lousy Kindergartener

We always hope that the lessons we teach our children are useful and used. It is somewhat humbling, however, when they show better understanding of the process than we do, leaving us to wonder who the parent is and who the child is, as this experience with my youngest as a kindergartener demonstrated.

My then six-year-old came home from kindergarten one day with a story of woe. She'd taken her Beanie Baby, Pattie the Platypus—the newest craze since Tickle Me Elmo—to school. During recess the platypus had fallen onto the pavement from her sock, having no pockets for storage. Another little girl grabbed it up and called it her own. Now, my daughter had, just that morning, put her initials on the tag for evidence of ownership. My daughter brought up this fact, hoping the issue could be easily resolved. The little girl refused to even look at the tag, simply stuffing Pattie in her pocket as she ran off.

If I had been my daughter, I would have chased her down, tackling her if necessary, to retrieve what was rightfully mine. *I would make a lousy kindergartener.* My daughter, so much wiser than her mother, chose instead to talk to a mutual friend of theirs. The mutual friend agreed to act as go-between to reunite my child with her beloved Beanie Baby. They agreed that if the item wasn't returned, my daughter would then report the incident to the teacher.

That night, my daughter told me about the incident and of the mutual friend who would talk with the other girl in the morning. I, *of little faith*, asked my daughter if it was okay if I called the girl's mother to help things along. I think I disappointed her slightly by not showing faith in her plan, but she decided that a little extra help wouldn't hurt. The mother was very friendly and understanding, checking with her daughter immediately about the whereabouts of Pattie Platypus, and assuring me that it would be returned the next morning. Hanging up, I felt better and my daughter was reassured that the matter was taken care of.

The next morning, while being dropped off at kindergarten, my daughter did ask me to let her teacher know, just in case the platypus wasn't returned. The teacher assured us she would assist— all my daughter had to do was to tell her. Happily, my daughter scampered off to play.

That evening, I entered the house excited to hear about the return of the platypus. Instead, my daughter said that the other girl had been too busy to return it. My daughter opted to give her till Monday (since we were into the weekend) to return it before enlisting the teacher's help. *I would make a lousy kindergartener.* I told my daughter that I would call the mother up and arrange, instead, for us to get the toy back over the weekend. I truly felt that the child was keeping Pattie the Platypus on purpose to torment my darling daughter. The family was gone, however, until late Sunday afternoon—learned from many encounters with their answering machine. My daughter had faith that once the girl realized it wasn't her Beanie Baby, she would return it. After all, she had her initials on the tag!

Finally, I was able to reach the mother. *This is where little faith gets you back.* The mother determined that her daughter had placed it in my daughter's backpack upon arriving at school that Friday. Wouldn't you know that we hadn't emptied out the bag over the weekend? For justification of my own actions, I reasoned that the girl hadn't let my child know of the return, so she was partially to blame for the added phone call. I apologized for bothering them and hung up. My daughter was ecstatic to have Pattie the Platypus back, and felt no ill feelings for the girl. She has decided, however, to leave it at home from now on. I probably would have wanted to stomp up to the other girl, yelling about ruining my weekend, worrying about my Beanie Baby, and why couldn't she have told me she'd put it in my backpack. *But after all, I would make a lousy kindergartener!*

CHAPTER 3

Dyslexia Is All In Your head

Understanding The Brain Differences

Sean's third-grade teacher constantly says, "Why can't a bright boy like you remember to check your work when writing?" Sean doesn't know "why" he can't—why he transposes letters in words, or words in sentences; why he can't distinguish between "b's," "d's," "p's," and "q's," or "u's" and "n's," or "m's" and "w's." Sean struggles with his homework, never right the first time. "What's wrong with my brain?" he frequently cries.

Sean struggles with the neurologic disorder dyslexia. Dyslexics are often mistakenly viewed as lazy, sloppy, or unmotivated by their parents and teachers, who see the contrasts of strengths and creativity with slow and uneven mastery of reading, spelling, writing, or math. Their work is marked by problems with organization, sloppy handwriting, and following instructions. Science is finding differences in the anatomy and functioning of the brain to answer Sean's question. The experts hope, as they learn more, to determine ways to identify dyslexia earlier and treat it more effectively.

Dyslexia is a neurologic disorder of the language systems of the brain. Fifteen percent of the population's affected by dyslexia, according to International Dyslexia from data collected by the National Institutes of Health and the US Department of Health, Education, and Welfare.

Dyslexia means difficulty with words. It affects a child's language in the area of phoneme awareness—hearing the units of sound making up each word. Reading and writing are visual representations of our language—the visual record of the spoken word. Every person learning to read and write needs to associate the individual sounds with the letters of the alphabet—symbols for our language sounds. Individuals with dyslexia, struggling with the initial acquisition of the sound elements, find that remembering the visual symbol is extremely difficult. Many children have a history of early language problems, ranging from articulation difficulties to expressive (word finding) language deficits. All of these findings point to specific areas of the brain that are affected.

There are several avenues of research worldwide being pursued to determine if there is one path leading to dyslexia, or several. Researchers in England have determined that there is a defective bridge between the front and back of the language areas of the brain. This created errors in their subjects when looking at phonics tasks and digit memory speed, a short-term memory task. In Finland, scientists studying adults with dyslexia determined that there is a deficit in the processing of rapid sound sequences with significant delays in their conscious awareness of auditory stimuli. This would suggest a similar difficulty with the processing of language, much like in the classroom.

Other researchers, such as at the National Institute of Mental Health (NIMH) in Bethesda, Maryland, in 1995, found deficits in the speed of processing of rapidly moving visual stimuli, again using adult dyslexics. In Tasmania, the Czech Republic, and Finland, other findings suggest a visual cause, along similar paths as the NIMH study. Many researchers are considering the possibility of dual pathways, with a common area of difficulty in the temporal lobe, which handles the speed of processing of information.

How does all of this explain the day-to-day difficulties of the child with dyslexia? Let's look at Jennifer as an example. Jennifer worked for hours on the one-page report, knowing, after complaints of sloppy written work and low test scores, it must be perfect for her to pass. Palms sweating, Jennifer offered her paper to Mr. Trousdale as he collected reports. His face changed to a scowl as he crushed up her paper, dropping it onto her desk. "Jennifer, you didn't even try to be neat or to follow the directions." Tears falling down her cheeks, Jennifer grabbed her books and stumbled out of the classroom.

Jennifer had found it difficult to keep up with Mr. Trousdale's oral directions, needing time to process the meaning of some words while maintaining the information in her short-term memory. Then there was the difficulty with keeping the directions in the correct order. During the preparation of the report, Jennifer had to reread the material several times in order to keep the sequence of information straight.

During the writing process, she had problems with remembering the spelling of the words, plus other rules of language, and finally instructing her hand in the formation of the letters, the spacing between words, and the placement of appropriate punctuation. Her work was marred by frequent erasures and crossing out of errors, poor penmanship, and incomplete thoughts.

A better understanding of the brain differences in dyslexia should afford hope to the Seans and Jennifers in our classes. By focusing on the language and visual areas of the brain, with some overlap in the fine motor area for writing, numerous accommodations and interventions can be provided, which will ease the strain as they learn in school. Methods that would help Sean and Jennifer include techniques by various professionals.

Suzanne Carreker, past president of the Houston Branch of the International Dyslexia Association, pointed out in her article, "Building Solid Foundations," that teaching phonological awareness required the following:

Systematic Training in Phonological Awareness. This is the direct instruction in hearing the units of sounds in words, not just single letters, but also syllables. Training in this area includes the following activities:

- Rhyming

- Counting words in a sentence

- Counting syllables

- Identifying sounds

- Counting sounds

- Omitting syllables in order to hear how it changes words.

Instant Letter Recognition. These are skills needed by the students for rapid identification of words, taught by the following activities:

- Reciting the alphabet

- Arranging plastic letters

- Playing guess what, requiring the child to close his eyes and then determine the plastic letter put into his hands

- Teaching the concept of before and after for letters.

A Solid Foundation for Comprehension. In order to understand what has been read, students needed to be taught, using the following activities:

- Reading aloud to the students by teachers, parents, and volunteers, in order to enrich their vocabulary

- Having the students talk about information relevant to the story read to them, focusing on setting, characters, and events

- Developing a verbal expression unit where a topic for the week is chosen, focusing each day on different aspects;

  □ naming, in general, things associated with the topic,

- naming by categories, and

- naming by attributes

- description of objects associated with the topic

- use of vocabulary relevant to the topic, including

- homonyms,

- synonyms, and

- idioms

• phonologic awareness

• preparing analogies that incorporate vocabulary and concepts related to the topic.

Ginger Holland, a regular education teacher, in her article, "Modifying the Regular Classroom," looked at the different areas of difficulty encountered by children with dyslexia. For each area, she developed a list of accommodations;

DIFFICULTY WITH HANDWRITING AND/OR COPYING

- Minimize copying from the board, worksheets, or books

- Allow the use of word processors

- Accept oral work as a substitute for written assignments

- Accept illustrations instead of words

DIFFICULTY WITH SPELLING

- Don't count spelling in reports and daily assignments

- Provide a word bank consisting of frequently used but misspelled words

- Allow students to use "the underline option" where they underline potentially misspelled words to check later

DIFFICULTY WITH READING

- Use highlighted or underlined reading materials

- Provide taped textbooks

- Allow someone to read to the student

DIFFICULTY WITH WRITTEN COMPOSITION

- Accept oral work as a substitute for written work

- Shorten written requirements

- Let the student dictate to another person

- Teach the child how to write a sentence, paragraph, and paper

- Be very specific about the expectations

HIGH ANXIETY IN TESTING SITUATIONS

- Give tests orally

- Allow more time

- Allow the test to be taken in a different environment

- Give shorter and more frequent tests

- Place fewer questions or problems on a page

- Reduce the number of items in matching tests

- Give multiple choice tests instead of objective tests

- Be aware of overall test readability

DIFFICULTY WITH THE CONCEPT
OF THE PASSAGE OF TIME

- Work out a system for modifications in homework to fit into a prescribed time of studying, e.g., ten minutes of homework per grade

- Reduce the amount of homework when possible

- Divide long-term assignments into stages with separate deadlines

- Maintain a calendar

POOR ORGANIZATIONAL SKILLS

- Encourage students to color-code textbooks, notebooks, and folders

- Teach the student how to keep an assignment notebook

- Monitor the assignment notebook

- Give preferential seating

SHORT ATTENTION SPAN

- Divide assignments into manageable parts

- Have a set procedure for the class

- Maintain the structure of the classroom

- Provide visual aids

- Provide concrete manipulatives

- Provide direct instructions

LOW SELF-ESTEEM

- Find something good to say each day

- Go easy on the red marks

- Watch for signs of progress

- Avoid saying, "This child is not trying"

All of these recommendations tap either directly into teaching the skills that are absent, or bypassing the deficits of dyslexia in order for the child to function on equal footing with his classmates. These are not unfair to the other children in the classroom, any more than glasses, a wheelchair, or a hearing aid give other students an advantage over the rest of a class. These are all tools to allow each student to show their skills, without barriers.

As we intervene and accommodate a child with dyslexia, we will have more time to also note his strengths. His creativity, his ability to see the world in three dimensions, rather than in two planes only, will begin to shine through. This has been evidenced by the careers of Whoopi Goldberg, Henry Winkler, Tom Cruise, Nelson Rockerfeller, and Agatha Christie, among many others.

Sammy gave his presentation on dinosaurs to the entire third-grade class. He presented it orally, augmented by his detailed illustrations of the animals, their habitat, and specific archeological dates, which had been printed on the poster board by his parents. His teacher had suggested this way of doing a report, knowing that he had much more to offer than his written skills suggested. She had also contacted The Recordings for the Blind and Dyslexics to aid him in his research, finding taped books on his subject. She had informed his family at the beginning of the year of the report, since it would take awhile to obtain the taped books, and Sammy deserved the time to do his best. Sammy is dyslexic and proud of it, recognizing his teacher's respect for his skills, not just noting his difficulties. He knows he is smart and that his brain is special. He can tell everyone that he is like Christopher Columbus. He knows the world is round, while nondyslexics think it is flat, as evidenced by written language. All he needs is the time to translate back and forth from the language of round to flat in order to function with his classmates. His mother often tells him she doubts many of his classmates are bilingual like he is, knowing the two languages. Yes, Sammy is dyslexic and proud of it.

CHAPTER 4

I Love You Because...

When you were born people around me began to grieve. They told me they were sorry about your problems, about the struggles you would have through life. They were sorry about the different life I would have because you were not the child they expected.

I, however, was thrilled to meet you. I loved you because I knew you would encourage me to be the best parent I could be. I loved you because you would force me to notice all the little steps it took to master "the simple things" in life. I loved you because you would help others realize how special life is.

As you have grown, you have taught me to love you because of the courage you have shown when faced with physical challenges. You have taught me to understand the intricacies of the human body and how many things can go wrong but can be "fixed".

I love you because you have taught me about how human beings develop. You have shown me how complex each developmental milestone is and why it is important to celebrate each step along the way.

I love you because you have shared with me the joys and sorrows of dealing with other people each day. You have shown me about ignorance, bias, and the inequalities of life. You have helped me to become an advocate for the rights of you and others.

I love you because you helped me see the people who also love without bias, without grief, without regrets. We have shared many important moments celebrating life with them.

I love you because you have attitude. This has shown me that struggles don't diminish a person's ability to have an opinion, have belief systems, and a desire to be independent, even as they need to be interdependent.

I love you because you gave me a life I would never have known to choose. A life outside of my comfort zone. A life where I am forced to notice each moment of each day in order to celebrate "the simple things" that others miss. A life where I am required to think of someone else other than myself. A life where I have to be creative in order to get from one place to another. You have expanded my skills and for that I am grateful.

I love you because you have loved me, despite my faults, flaws, and imperfections. I thank God every day that he allowed me to be your parent.

CHAPTER 5

The Gift of Time

"Hurry up! Why do you have to take so long to do everything?" "You need to use your time more wisely." "He always hurries through his work, making careless mistakes."

These are frequent comments that children with processing problems hear. Unfortunately, they don't reflect why these children are struggling. None of these children want to have this negative type of impression of who they are. They don't stay up late nights, or get up early to think of ways to get in trouble or to disappoint the adults in their lives. It just happens naturally!

According to the World Health Organization (WHO), one child in every six has some type of neurodevelopmental disorder. All children with neurodevelopmental disorders have processing problems which have a direct impact on their ability to learn and function in their worlds. We need to understand what these processing issues are and how to help so that we don't just "Assume" why they don't meet our day-to-day expectations.

All processing starts with our senses—hearing, seeing, feeling, etc. Our nerves pick up a sensory signal, transporting the information to our brains, which then determines what it means and what to do with it. All of this takes time. If a child's brain has problems in the processing of the information coming in, it takes longer to process it, and then determine what to do with the information. Instead of milliseconds, it may take several seconds, to even more than a minute to complete the steps needed for a response (which is called output).

Stress has a very negative effect on processing ability. Just consider what you feel like when you are on a deadline, or are running late, and people keep putting more demands on you. Have you ever shouted "Be quiet. I can't think when you keep talking!" And, if you are lucky, this only happens occasionally. Imagine if this is your life every day, from the time you get up to the time you go to bed. Wouldn't you love to be given the gift of time?

What can you do to give this gift of time to the children you work or live with who are experiencing developmental or behavioral challenges? First, present information in small steps. If you have several steps that need to be completed, give one direction at a time, allowing the child to finish it first. Then give the second direction, and so on until the task is completed. This also allows you to provide the child with positive reinforcement on their compliance and motivation to be successful.

Second, this presentation would be best presented in a combined visual/verbal format. Auditory processing is a major problem for even average individuals, but for these children it is a severe problem. Backing it up with visuals allows for improvement in understanding, processing, storing, and retrieval of information later. Presenting in one-step formats, allows for mastering of the information before adding demands to it.

Third, allow extended time to process what you have presented. The amount of time is determined by watching the child and his rate of change from looking/listening to either question asking, or the beginning of a motor action to give you what you asked for. From that watching, begin to set up that amount of time naturally, with a shortening as the child shows that he can complete the process faster. Using timed math tests as an example, first see how many items that he can complete in the allotted time. Note how many he accurately answered in that timeframe. Then adjust the timeframe for him to be able to complete the test. As he becomes more efficient in his processing, note how much sooner he can complete the set of problems until he can do it in the same timeframe as his classmates.

An important point to remember is that you are not being unfair to the other children who are in your life by doing this. You are being totally fair, in that for each child who needs an individualized intervention to be on the same playing field for task mastery, you are providing what is needed. Making every child do (and expecting every child to do) tasks the same way, in the same time frame, etc. is being equal, not fair (thanks to Richard Lavoie for introducing me to this difference). What if everyone had to wear a red dress of the same size and style, whether they looked good in it, whether it fit or not, or whether they were male or female. Would that be "fair"? No, it would be equal but definitely not fair.

How much time should you give? Simple answer—as much as he needs. You may need to alter your expectations of what is needed to complete a task. Or you may need to build in more accommodations to allow the child to complete it in a timeframe that better suits your needs. Some children, and adults, will never be able to complete some tasks in the timeline that is needed if they are not provided with accommodations. But, that is what technology has been able to give many individuals with processing problems. Calculators allow individuals with math processing problems to come up with answers much faster than they would have been able to in a time crunch situation. Accounting software allows people to keep track of their finances and to budget more effectively, when they wouldn't have been able to keep track of this information otherwise.

Bottom line, if it becomes apparent that a person's processing problems will always create stress, bring in accommodations to allow him to have time for the rest of his lives. The most precious gift we can give to each other is the gift of time. It will add to the quality of our lives and allow us to share our time with those we care about most.

IN CLOSING

I have shared with you only a snippet of the experiences that I have had with children and what they have taught me about how to best be their teacher, mentor, coach, friend, and parent. As you spend time just sitting and watching, listening to, and enjoying your child, remember that they want to be part of our lives. After all, despite what we may feel some days, they don't get up in the morning and put at the top of their to-do list (or anywhere on it for that matter) "Find ways to get my parents mad at me and force them to punish me." Kids only want to be loved, respected, and accepted. The rest we have to teach them.

APPENDIX

TEMPERAMENT:

Resources:

Internet: www.b-di.com. This site has a newsletter that you can sign up for on raising the high-maintenance child.

Books:

Parents: The Difficult Child by Stanley Turecki, MD. This is a classic resource for parents and professionals. He describes in detail the different traits with suggestions on how to work with each trait.

Raising Your Spirited Child by Mary Sheedy Kurcinka. This is another classic that also has a workbook to walk you through possible scenarios with low-stress results.

Professionals working with children:
Coping with Children's Temperament by William Carey, MD, and Sean McDevitt, PhD.

Temperament in Clinical Practice, by Stella Chess, MD and Alexander Thomas, MD.

Temperament in the Classroom by Barbara Keogh, PhD.

The Temperament Perspective by Jan Kristal, MA.

The Long Shadow of Temperament, by Jerome Kagan & Nancy Snidman

RESPECT:

Resources:
How to Talk So Kids Will Listen, and Listen So Kids Will Talk by Adele Faber and Elaine Mazlish.

Systematic Training for Effective Parenting by Don Dinkmeyer and Gary McKay.

RESOURCES FOR INDIVIDUALS WITH LEARNING DISABILITIES

Children and adults with learning disabilities often feel isolated. Many don't know where to turn for help, either in the form of accommodations or technology. Below are several contact resources to decrease the sense of isolation and confusion.

INTERNATIONAL DYSLEXIA ASSOCIATION

40 York Rd., 4th Floor
Baltimore, MD 21204
Voice: (410) 296-0232
Fax: (410) 321-5069
E-mail: info@interdys.org
Web Site: http://www.interdys.org

LEARNING DISABILITIES ASSOCIATION (LDA)

4156 Library Road
Pittsburgh, PA 15234-1349
Phone: (412) 341-1515

Fax: (412) 344-0224

Web Site: http://www.ldanatl.org

THE NATIONAL CENTER FOR LEARNING DISABILITIES (NCLD)

381 Park Avenue South, Suite 1401

New York, NY 10016

Phone: (212) 545-7510

Fax: (212) 545-9665

Toll-free: (888) 575-7373

Web Site: http://www.ncld.org

LEARNING ALLY (FORMERLY RECORDINGS FOR THE BLIND AND DYSLEXICS)

20 Roszel Road

Princeton, NJ 08540

Phone: 609-750-1830

(Member Services): (800) 221-4792

Q.E.D FOUNDATION (THEY ACQUIRED ALL KINDS OF MINDS)

105 State Route 101A, Unit 1A
Amherst, NH 03031
(603) 589-9517
Fax: (603) 589-9518
www.QEDfoundation.org

How can you use this book?

MOTIVATE

EDUCATE

THANK

INSPIRE

PROMOTE

CONNECT

Why have a custom version of *Never Assume*?

- Build personal bonds with customers, prospects, employees, donors, and key constituencies

- Develop a long-lasting reminder of your event, milestone, or celebration

- Provide a keepsake that inspires change in behavior and change in lives

- Deliver the ultimate "thank you" gift that remains on coffee tables and bookshelves

- Generate the "wow" factor

Books are thoughtful gifts that provide a genuine sentiment that other promotional items cannot express. They promote employee discussions and interaction, reinforce an event's meaning or location, and they make a lasting impression. Use your book to say "Thank You" and show people that you care.

Never Assume is available in bulk quantities and in customized versions at special discounts for corporate, institutional, and educational purposes. To learn more please contact our Special Sales team at:

1.866.775.1696 • sales@advantageww.com • wwwAdvantageSpecialSales.com